Wild Wor

Animal Helpers

by Dr. Jim Flegg with
Eric & David Hosking

Belitha Press

People co-operate to control a fire.

Title page: *a band of dwarf mongooses on a termite hill.*

Contents

Animal Helpers	3
Team Hunters	4
Living Cities	8
Social Harmony	10
Defending the Herd	14
Housekeeping Help	16
Hitching a Lift	20
Helpful to People	21
Glossary	24

Front cover: *A family group of black-faced vervet monkeys.*
Back cover: *A pride of lions.*

Animal Helpers

We often think of 'helping' as a very human activity. Lending a helping hand is something that we are able to do because of our well-developed brains and social structure. We think that nature tends to exclude helping in the battle for survival. This is far from being the case. Though giving unselfish help of the sort we call charity – fund raising for disaster relief, for example – does not seem to be part of the animal scene, the Wild World *does* contain social helpers. This help can be as varied as babysitting, hairdressing, and providing food for nursing mothers. Many animal communities join together to gather food, whether it be honey, cereals or meat, in just the same way as human villagers do, whether Inuit (Eskimos) hunting seals or South Sea islanders gathering coconuts. No human society could function without the help and co-operation of its members.

What does 'help' mean in the Wild World? The answers are many and surprising. We find not only ant communities with nursemaids, food gatherers and soldiers working together to ensure the success of the colony, but also colonial jellyfish organized in much the same way. There are animals that team up to help others of their kind in defence, or that hunt as a pack to feed their clan. There are insects and birds that act as foster parents to others of their kind – though they may not get much reward for doing so. There are also examples of one animal helping to transport another. Animals may help plants in **pollination**. They may even help people – from earthworms acting as nature's ploughs to vultures as nature's dustmen!

Nesting kittiwakes.

A swarm of bees.

Lionesses and their cubs feast on a freshly-killed zebra.

Team Hunters

Some animals co-operate to find food, and even some of the fiercest and strongest find it better to hunt together rather than alone. In a group of lions – called a 'pride' – it is not the massive, heavily maned male that does the hunting, but the lionesses. Each pride will usually have only one mature male, who will have several full-grown lionesses in his pride. These lionesses help the pride by hunting as a team. Sometimes several form a line to drive a herd of antelope or zebra, or perhaps a warthog family, forward. One or two other lionesses lie in wait, well hidden behind rocks or bushes, ready to ambush the fleeing animals. Panic-stricken by the pursuing lionesses, the terrified **prey** animals abandon caution in their desperate need to escape and run straight into the waiting claws and jaws of the ambushing lionesses.

The terrifying howling of wolves may be a frequent feature of horror films, but actual wolf attacks on people are very rare indeed. In Northern Europe, reindeer are the wolf's major **prey.** Wolves are pack animals, with a well-organized team structure. Usually an individual reindeer is selected from the herd as the pack's victim, and then relentlessly pursued. Various wolves take turns to take the lead, so that the endurance of the pack is sustained over the marathon chase. All the pack help in the kill but there the co-operation ends. Only when the chief male and his favourite bitches and their cubs have eaten their fill can the junior members of the pack come to feed.

Wolves are very social animals.

Baboons are hunter-gatherers. They feed on roots and fruit, and on any small animals that they find, from grasshoppers and lizards to birds' eggs. They travel as a troop, spending most of the time on the ground. Youngsters will often ride on an older baboon, sitting on its back like a jockey as it walks on all four legs through the **bush**. Baboon troops **forage** for food as a team, the mothers and young baboons sharing what they find. The senior and strongest male is their leader. In just the same way as soldiers salute their officers, grooming and grins and snarls show that all baboon troop members know who is in charge. Baboons have brightly coloured bottoms. These give messages to the whole troop, showing who is top male (the most colourful) and who are his favourite females. Baboon troops always have a sentry. At a bark of alarm, youngsters and females rush to safety in the trees, the young being helped by any nearby older baboon. Defence of the troop is left to the males. They have huge mouths well-armed with teeth, able even to drive off a leopard.

A baboon troop leader relaxes with his favourite females.

Brown pelicans on a fishing expedition.

With their waddling walk pelicans are clumsy on land, but they are majestic when soaring in flight and are expert fishermen. Equipped with a huge pouched beak to trap fish, many pelicans use team-work to increase their catch. Several birds will swim along in horseshoe formation, like a fleet of galleons under full sail, driving the fish before them. Then, with the precision timing of a troupe of ballet dancers, the leading birds bring the arms of the horseshoe together to form a ring. In unison they dip their huge beaks deep under water to scoop up the fish they have surrounded, raising their wings to keep their balance. Learning from the birds, human fishermen often use the same encircling technique with their nets.

The tentacles of this Portuguese man-o'-war have captured a fish.

Living Cities

Jellyfish are usually thought of as lowly marine animals, uncomplicated in structure and lacking the sophisticated and powerful resources of successful hunters like sharks. The notorious Portuguese man-o'-war is far from simple. In fact it is not actually a jellyfish at all. It is a colony of animals, all the same species but each different in shape and depending on the assistance of the others for survival. One is a melon-sized floating bladder that drifts along, blown by the wind. From this hang others, some the reproductive organs of the colony, others its mouths taking in and digesting fish caught by the stinging tentacles, which are also colony members. These are covered with **microscopic** poison darts packing a punch capable of killing fish and even human swimmers. This lethal net is spread over several metres. The Portuguese man-o'-war is like a floating city in which each member is helpless without the others.

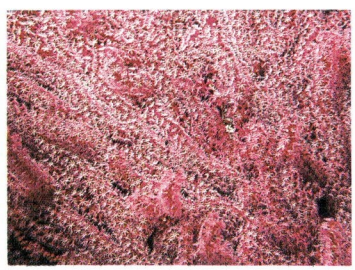

The hard, rough corals that form the massive ship-wrecking reefs that encircle some ocean islands, and that create beautiful underwater **zoological** gardens like the Great Barrier Reef off eastern Australia, are the chalky skeletons of co-operative colonies of tiny animals. These corals may be wonderfully varied in shape. Some look like deer antlers, some like toadstools, some like ferns, and a few are rare and beautiful enough to be made into jewellery. The colony has a communal skin covering the skeleton. This contains the cells that build the coral, and tiny animals called **polyps**, like miniature sea anemones. Some polyps have tentacles and do the feeding, others are simpler and help by pumping food and water through the colony. Tiny though the individual polyps may be, working together over time they can create reefs larger than any harbour-building scheme ever attempted by human engineers.

Devonshire cup coral – above *are some hard coral polyps.*

9

Ants guard their eggs carefully – they represent the future of the colony.

Social Harmony

Though ants are small creatures, what they lack in size they more than make up for in organization. An ants' nest normally holds many thousands of individuals. Chief among them is the queen, larger than her subjects and bloated because she spends her life doing little else but eat and lay eggs. Male ants – the princes – appear only occasionally, and once they have mated with a queen their life is over. The rest of the colony are workers. Some species have members with specially armoured heads and jaws. These are the soldiers whose job is to defend the colony. Others are food gatherers, roaming far and wide to harvest food for the colony. Yet others may look after **aphids** on plants, protecting and tending them just as human farmers keep herds of cows and sheep. The ants 'milk' the aphids each day for the sugary liquids that they produce. All these rich foods are fed to the growing ant youngsters deep down in the nest by nursemaid ants.

Most blue butterfly caterpillars have a honey gland on their back. Ants find the sugary liquid that it produces delicious, and they 'milk' the caterpillars by stroking the gland with their feet or **antennae**. The ants help the caterpillars by carrying them to fresh food plants when necessary, and guard them from **parasitic** wasp attacks. At the end of the summer, the ants carry the caterpillars down into their underground nest. Here they live through the winter by feeding on ant **larvae**. In the following spring, they **pupate** and emerge as jewels amongst the butterflies.

An adonis blue butterfly.

A chimpanzee mother with her babies.

Chimpanzees keep clean by grooming each other.

These chimpanzee males are challenging each other.

Though not the largest of the 'great apes', chimpanzees are possibly the most intelligent of them. Once it was thought that chimpanzees were vegetarians, but now we know that they include a good deal of meat in their diet. In fact their lifestyle of 'hunter-gatherers' is very similar to that of the earliest cavemen. Chimps have hands just like ours, with a thumb that can be used, with the fingertips, to pick up even the most delicate and tiny things. This ability is special to man and the apes. Chimps also use their nimble fingers to comb through one another's long hair. Called grooming, this helps them keep their hair tidy – just as a visit to the hairdresser does for us. Fleas, lice and ticks are a problem in the African forests, as are burr-like plant seeds. By grooming each other, they can be sure that all the difficult-to-reach areas are regularly inspected. Grooming also encourages social contact. It's a great way for members of the troop to get to know each other. Junior chimps in the troop are able to show their respect for their leaders by combing their hair. So besides giving pleasure, grooming is also a means of communication, an animal alternative to words.

Defending the Herd

Musk oxen are tough. They live closer to the North Pole than any other grazing animal, protected from the cold by a thick fleece with hairs up to 70 centimetres long. Solidly built, they stand only 150 centimetres high at the shoulder, but may weigh almost half a tonne. Both males and females have massive horns, long, curved and sharply pointed, with thick bases to protect the skull. Musk ox herds have a well-developed defensive strategy, effective even against wolves. They gather in a tight group, facing their enemy. An impressive array of horns points outwards and the calves shelter behind. Winter herds may contain fifty animals – only a desperately hungry wolf pack would attack such formidable defences.

A group of musk oxen on the Arctic tundra.

A mother elephant helps up her baby.

All the female elephants in a group will give help to any youngster, pushing over trees so that they can reach tender leaves, or using their trunks to assist them up a steep slope. Trunks are also just as good as hands when it comes to smacking naughty behinds! Although no animal would seem less likely to be attacked than the massive African elephant, young ones are at risk from lions and hyenas, especially if they stray far from their mother. If danger threatens, all the female elephants – mothers, sisters, cousins and aunts – gather in a tight circle with the young grouped safely in the middle. Attackers face a fearsome ring of long, sharp white tusks. An elephant rolls up its trunk and tucks it back between its tusks, out of harm's way when it charges. This is the danger sign to watch out for! Even so, it can still produce a terrifying squealing and trumpeting that brings other elephants thundering to help at an amazing turn of speed.

Housekeeping Help

▌Many of the larger animals that roam the African plains, such as antelopes, zebras, rhinos, buffaloes and giraffes often have oxpeckers for company. The nimble oxpecker can move quickly about all over its travelling **host**. For much of the time they are a help to their hosts – they are quick to spot danger and sound the alarm, and they pick off irritating ticks and excavate maggots from the animal's tough skin. The plain's animals happily accept this service until the oxpecker goes too far! Finding an open sore, they use their sharp beaks to snip off pieces of living flesh, to the discomfort of their host, which gallops off in an attempt to dislodge its painful visitor.

An oxpecker perches on an African buffalo.

▌Most members of the heron and egret family are waterside birds, using their long legs to wade out into deep water and their long necks and sharp, dagger-like beaks to grab or stab passing fish, frogs, and the occasional unwary bird. The cattle egret is the exception. More often than not it is found far from water in company with grazing animals, not just cattle but also wild elephant, buffalo and antelopes. As they move across the grassy plains, herds of these large animals disturb countless grasshoppers and other large insects, and the occasional juicy small lizard. Keeping close by the feet of its helper, the cattle egret is well placed to snap up an easy meal.

Cattle egrets.

Ruppell's griffon vultures feed on a dead zebra.

A heaving mass of blood-stained vultures fighting silently over the leftovers from a lion's kill might seem a revolting sight. But in clearing up this **carrion**, rotting fast in the tropical sun, the vultures are performing a vital service for other animals, including humans, by removing a source of disease. The bigger vultures are among the largest of flying birds, with broad wings spanning up to three metres. They soar effortlessly at great heights, riding on rising currents of hot air. Vultures have spectacularly good eyesight and can spot likely food from one thousand metres or more.

Meerkats are among the smaller members of the mongoose family. Few animals are so well organized. Meerkat groups, often up to twenty strong, are family clans. Clan chief is the dominant male, who has his favourite old females. Younger males and females go out to hunt for the whole clan, while some males act as lookouts. A continuous guard is vital, as their home in the African **bush** teems with **predators** as stealthy as snakes, or as sudden as hawks plunging out of the blue skies. Standing upright, the sentry yelps an alarm if danger threatens, and all the meerkats scuttle for cover down their burrows. If the danger is a snake the older males circle and attack it. The meerkat is nimble, and has reflexes fast enough to dodge a striking cobra. Meanwhile, the babysitters – the 'teenagers' of the clan – hastily collect up the babies in their mouths and carry them off to a fresh hideout.

Meerkats are always on the alert.

The reed warbler is dwarfed by the cuckoo chick in its nest.

Each spring, cuckoos fly north from the tropics to the reed beds of Europe where they will breed. Each female patrols her own territory, keeping a secretive watch on the reed warbler nests. Just as the reed warbler finishes laying her clutch of eggs, the cuckoo pays a lightning-fast visit to the nest to lay an egg that looks just like the reed warbler's. The egg soon hatches, and the muscular young cuckoo that emerges quickly pushes its foster parents' eggs or chicks out over the side of the nest. The cuckoo chick grows rapidly and soon dwarfs its foster parents. Its demands for food keep the weary reed warblers busy from dawn till dusk. The fact that the cuckoo **fledgling** does not demolish the nest is a tribute to the nest-building skills of the unsuspecting reed warbler, which unwittingly helps the cuckoo by playing foster parent to its greedy chick.

Hitching a Lift

Many of the larger ground beetles, like this monster, lumber around like slow-moving six-legged armoured cars, though nevertheless covering a surprising amount of ground. So slow-moving are they that much smaller, less mobile animals are able to use the beetles as a bus service. Here a number of ginger-coloured mites (tiny eight-legged relatives of the spiders, so small as to be clearly visible only through a magnifying glass) have hitched a ride on a rhinoceros beetle. They will do it no harm, are certainly not heavy to carry, and they find it easy to get a foothold on the elaborate armour plating of the beetle's head and shoulders.

The head of a rhinoceros beetle with mites hanging on around its mouth.

A bumble-bee collecting pollen.

Helping People

▯ Some flowers are **pollinated** by the wind, but many depend on insects to carry **pollen** from one flower to fertilize another so that the seed or fruit can grow. Evolution has given these flowers bright colours and sometimes a strong scent to attract pollinating insects. Bees, like this bumble-bee, are the most important pollinators. For them, the 'reward' for their help in pollination is nectar, a sugary liquid that the bees use as food. Bumble-bees work on their own, but worker honey-bees help direct others from their hive to good sources of nectar by performing a dance to show in which direction they must fly. Of about 20,000 species of bee, only a handful are true honey-bees. Workers inside the hive convert the gathered nectar into sugar-rich honey, an excellent food (for bees as well as humans) to feed them through the winter.

▯ Honeyguides are drab, sparrow-sized African birds. They feed mostly on the honey, wax and grubs in honey-bees' nests. The greater honey-guide has developed the most amazing habit of helping the honey badger, another honey-hunting animal, and even African tribesmen by leading them to bees' nests. Calling frequently as it flies through the trees ahead of the honey seeker the honeyguide waits impatiently to feed on the left-overs.

A honeyguide.

Taken all together, the earthworms that live below a grassy meadow weigh more than all the cattle or sheep that graze above ground. Earthworms are the single most important factor in maintaining the **fertility** of our soils, vital to successful crop growth. Their deep burrows let in air for the soil **microbes** to breathe. They also carry rainwater to the deeper layers, and at the same time work as drainpipes when flooding threatens. Earthworms eat leaves that they drag down from the surface, and excrete a finely powdered **nutrient**-rich material called humus. This is then used by growing plants, completing nature's recycling of organic fertilizers.

Earthworms play a valuable part in keeping soil fertile.

Worms turned up by the plough make an easy meal for these gulls.

Gulls are probably the most successful birds of the 20th century. One hundred years ago, gulls would only appear near towns during stormy weather at sea, but today they are commonplace, resting on **urban** parks and playing fields. Huge flocks feed on rubbish dumps, roosting overnight on nearby reservoirs. In the breeding season, many gulls now nest on rooftops rather than cliffs, producing a mess and a noisy dawn chorus that greatly reduces their popularity. The secret of their success is adaptability – their ability to make the most of the help unknowingly offered by humans. They exploit our parks, live off our waste food, and even follow close behind the farmland tractor to catch worms exposed by the plough.

Glossary

antennae (singular = antenna) organs on the heads of insects and other animals such as crabs; used for smelling and touching 11

aphids tiny insects that live on plants, often doing great damage 10

bush wild, uncultivated land not settled on by people 6, 18

carrion the dead bodies of animals 17

fertility the quality of being fertile, being fruitful and productive 22

fledgling a young bird that has just developed its feathers and will soon leave its nest 19

forage to wander around in search of food 6

host an animal or plant that has a *parasite* or other plant or animal living on it 16

larva (plural = larvae) the grub form of an insect from the time it leaves the egg until it becomes a pupa (when it changes into an adult insect) 11

microbe a very small living thing, either plant or animal, that can only be seen using a microscope 22

microscopic something so small that it can only be seen using a microscope 8

nutrient something that provides nourishment 22

parasitic living in or on another plant or animal and taking nourishment directly from it, or depending on another plant or animal for nourishment. A plant or animal that lives like this is called a parasite 11

pollen a fine powdery substance produced by the male part of flowers that must be taken to the female part of flowers so that seeds or fruit may grow 21

pollination the taking of *pollen* from one flower to another by wind or insects or other animals so that seeds or fruit may grow 3, 21

polyps simple small animals that have tubelike bodies attached to a base of some sort at one end and a mouth surrounded by tentacles or arms at the other 9

predator an animal that lives by hunting other animals for food 18

prey an animal that is killed and eaten by another animal 4, 5

pupate to become a pupa; the stage of an insect's life when it changes into an adult 11

urban being in or part of a town or city 23

zoological belonging to the study of animals 9

First published in Great Britain in 1990 by Belitha Press Limited
31 Newington Green, London N16 9PU
Text copyright © Dr. Jim Flegg 1990
Photographs copyright © David and Eric Hosking and the Frank Lane Picture Agency 1990 and individual copyright holders on the following pages: J. Bastable 20, C. Carvalho 9 (top), A. Christiansen 5, Treat Davidson 3, D. Dugan 2, F. Hartmann (title page), G. E. Hyde 21, Steve McCutcheon 14, Chris Newton 11, R. van Nostrand 18, Fritz Polking (cover), 16, Michael Rose 22, Silvestris 6, 12 (both), Terry Whittaker 15, D. P. Wilson 8, 9 (bottom)

Editor/Art Director: Treld Bicknell
Associate Editor: Robert Snedden
Design: Cathy Barrett
All rights reserved. No part of this book may be reproduced or utilized in any form or by any means, electronic or mechanical, including photocopying, recording or by any information storage and retrieval system, without permission in writing from the Publisher.
Printed in the UK for Imago Publishing
British Library Cataloguing in Publication Data for this book is available from the British Library.
ISBN 1 85561 004 3